THEY HAVE A PLENTIFUL

*lack of wit*

HAMLET, ACT 2, SCENE 2

HIS WIT'S AS

THICK AS A

*tewkesbury*

*mustard*

IF THOU WILT NEEDS MARRY,

*marry a fool;*

FOR WISE MEN KNOW

WELL ENOUGH

WHAT MONSTERS

YOU MAKE OF THEM.

HAMLET, ACT 3, SCENE 1

THOU DAMNED

AND LUXURIOUS

*mountain*

*goat*

HENRY V, ACT 4, SCENE 4

YOUR ABILITIES

ARE TOO INFANT-LIKE

FOR DOING MUCH ALONE.

CORIOLANUS, ACT 2, SCENE 1

*foul spoken*

*coward,*

THAT THUND'REST

WITH THY TONGUE,

AND WITH THY WEAPON

NOTHING DARES PERFORM.

*thou*

*sodden-witten*

*lord!*

THOU HAST NO MORE BRAIN

THAN I HAVE IN MINE ELBOWS!

TROILUS AND CRESSIDA, ACT 2, SCENE 1

MORE OF

YOUR CONVERSATION WOULD

*infect my*

*brain*

YOUR BRAIN IS AS DRY

AS THE REMAINDER BISCUIT

AFTER VOYAGE.

AS YOU LIKE IT, ACT 2, SCENE 7

IF YOU SPEND

WORD FOR WORD WITH ME,

I SHALL MAKE YOUR WIT

*bankrupt*

TWO GENTLEMEN OF VERONA, ACT 2, SCENE 4

THOU ART THE CAP OF

*all the fools*

HE HAS

NOT SO MUCH BRAIN AS

*ear wax*

TROILUS AND CRESSIDA ACT 5, SCENE 1

*whoreson*

*caterpillars,*

BACON-FED KNAVES!

HENRY IV PART I, ACT 2, SCENE 2

THERE'S SMALL CHOICE IN

*rotten apples*

AWAY THOU RAG,

THOU QUANTITY,

THOU REMNANT.

HE TAMING OF THE SHREW, ACT 4, SCENE 3

GO, PRICK THY FACE,

AND OVER-RED THY FEAR,

THOU LILY-LIVER'D BOY.

VILLAIN,

I HAVE DONE

THY MOTHER.

YOU, MINION,

ARE TOO

*Saucy*

THE TWO GENTLEMEN OF VERONA, ACT 1,

AWAY, YOU

*mouldy*

*rogue,*

AWAY!

I MUST TELL YOU

FRIENDLY IN YOUR EAR,

SELL WHEN YOU CAN,

YOU ARE NOT

FOR ALL MARKETS.

AS YOU LIKE IT, ACT 3, SCENE 5

I SCORN YOU,

*Scurvy*

*Companion*

HENRY IV, PART 2, ACT 2, SCENE 4

THIS WOMAN'S

AN EASY GLOVE,

MY LORD,

SHE GOES OFF AND ON

AT PLEASURE.

ALL'S WELL THAT ENDS WELL, ACT 5

WAS THE DUKE A

FLESH-MONGER,

A FOOL AND

A COWARD?

*thou*

*whoreson zed,*

THOU UNNECESSARY LETTER!

KING LEAR, ACT 2, SCENE 2

YOU ARE NOT WORTH

ANOTHER WORD,

ELSE I'D CALL YOU KNAVE.

THY SIN'S NOT ACCIDENTAL,

BUT A TRADE.

MEASURE FOR MEASURE, ACT 3, SCENE 1

A FOOL,

AN EMPTY PURSE.

THERE WAS NO MONEY IN'T.

THY TONGUE OUTVENOMS

ALL THE

*worms of*

*the Nile*

CYMBELINE, ACT 3, SCENE 4

WOULD THOU WERT CLEAN

ENOUGH TO SPIT UPON.

I DO DESIRE

THAT WE MAY BE BETTER

*strangers*

AS YOU LIKE IT, ACT 3, SCENE 2

AWAY, YOU STARVELLING,

YOU ELF-SKIN,

YOU DRIED NEAT'S-TONGUE,

BULL'S-PIZZLE,

YOU STOCK-FISH!

*Bloody,*

BAWDY VILLAIN!

REMORSELESS,

TREACHEROUS,

LECHEROUS,

KINDLESS VILLAIN!

HAMLET, ACT 2, SCENE 2

YOU ARE AS A CANDLE,

THE BETTER BURNT OUT

HENRY IV PART 2, ACT 1, SCENE 2

YOU ARE NOW SAILED

INTO THE NORTH OF

MY LADY'S OPINION,

WHERE YOU WILL HANG

LIKE AN ICICLE

ON A DUTCHMAN'S BEARD.

EATER OF

*broken*

*meats*

THREADBARE

*juggler*

THE COMEDY OF ERRORS, ACT 5, SCENE 1

*Saucy*

LACKEY!

HEAVEN TRULY KNOWS

THAT THOU ART

*false*

*as*

*hell*

OTHELLO, ACT 4, SCENE 2

*dissembling harlot,*

THOU ART FALSE IN ALL.

THE COMEDY OF ERRORS, ACT 4, SCENE 4

THOU SUBTLE,

PERJUR'D,

FALSE,

*disloyal*

*man*

THOU LEATHERN-JERKIN,

CRYSTAL-BUTTON,

KNOT-PATED,

AGATERING,

PUKE-STOCKING,

CADDIS-GARTER,

SMOOTH-TONGUE,

SPANISH POUCH!

HENRY IV PART 1, ACT 2, SCENE 4

THERE'S NO MORE

FAITH IN THEE

THAN IN A

*stewed*

*prune*

*I do wish thou were a dog,*

THAT I MIGHT

LOVE THEE SOMETHING.

TIMON OF ATHENS, ACT 4, SCENE 4

THINE FORWARD VOICE,

NOW, IS TO SPEAK WELL OF

THINE FRIEND;

THINE BACKWARD VOICE

IS TO UTTER FOUL SPEECHES

AND TO DETRACT.

WHAT A

THRICE-DOUBLE ASS!

IT IS A TALE

*told by*

*an idiot*

FULL OF SOUND AND FURY,

SIGNIFYING NOTHING.

MACBETH, ACT 5, SCENE 5

THOU CREAM FACED

MACBETH. ACT 5, SCENE 3

WHAT AN ASS!

HAMLET, ACT 2, SCENE 2

*a weasel*

HATH NOT SUCH A DEAL OF

SPLEEN AS YOU

ARE TOSS'D WITH

*poisonous*

BUNCH-BACKED TOAD!

RICHARD III, ACT 1, SCENE 3

HERE IS THE BABE,

AS LOATHSOME AS

*a toad*

TITUS ANDRONICUS, ACT 4, SCENE 2

LIKE THE TOAD;

*ugly and*

*venomous*

A RARE

PARROT-TEACHER!

MUCH ADO ABOUT NOTHING, ACT 1, SCENE 1

BOTTLED SPIDER!

RICHARD III, ACT 1, SCENE 3

COME, COME, YOU

FROWARD AND UNABLE

*worms*

PIGEON-LIVER'D

*lack gall*

HAMLET, ACT 2, SCENE 2

she hath
more hair
than wit,

AND MORE FAULTS

THAN HAIRS,

AND MORE WEALTH

THAN FAULTS.

TWO GENTLEMEN OF VERONA, ACT 3, SCENE 1

NO LONGER FROM

HEAD TO FOOT THAN

FROM HIP TO HIP,

SHE IS SPHERICAL,

LIKE A GLOBE,

I COULD FIND OUT

COUNTRIES IN HER.

THE COMEDY OF ERRORS, ACT 3, SCENE 2

YOU HAVE SUCH A

FEBRUARY FACE,

SO FULL OF FROST,

OF STORM AND

*cloudiness*

OUT OF MY SIGHT!

THOU DOST

*infect*

*my eyes*

*I am sick*

WHEN I DO

LOOK ON THEE

A MIDSUMMER NIGHT'S DREAM. ACT 2

THOU ELVISH-MARK'D,

ABORTIVE,

ROOTING HOG!

RICHARD III, ACT 1, SCENE 3

*thou art*
*a boil,*

A PLAGUE SORE,

AN EMBOSSED CARBUNCLE

IN MY CORRUPTED BLOOD.

KING LEAR, ACT 2, SCENE 4

THE RANKEST COMPOUND

OF VILLAINOUS SMELL

THAT EVER

*offended*

*nostril*

*the tartness*

*of his face*

SOURS RIPE GRAPES

THE COMEDY OF ERRORS ACT 5, SCENE 4

HER FACE IS NOT WORTH

*sunburning*

HENRY V, ACT 5, SCENE 2

THOU ART AS

*fat as*

*butter*

O YOU BEAST!

I'LL SO MAUL YOU

AND YOUR TOASTING-IRON,

THAT YOU SHALL THINK

THE DEVIL IS

COME FROM HELL.

KING JOHN, ACT 4, SCENE 3

I'LL BEAT THEE,

BUT I WOULD

*infect*

*my hands*

BY MINE HONOUR,

IF I WERE BUT

TWO HOURS YOUNGER,

I'D BEAT THEE.

METHINK'ST THOU ART

A GENERAL OFFENCE,

AND EVERY MAN

SHOULD BEAT THEE.

ALL'S WELL THAT ENDS WELL, ACT 2

WOULD THOU

WOULDST BURST!

TIMON OF ATHENS, ACT 4, SCENE 3

THOU

HATEFUL

WITHER'D

HAG!

YOU SHOULD BE WOMEN,

AND YET YOUR BEARDS

FORBID ME TO INTERPRET

THAT YOU ARE SO

MACBETH, ACT 1, SCENE 3

MY WIFE'S A

*hobby*

*horse*

YOU POOR,

BASE,

RASCALLY,

CHEATING

LACK-LINEN MATE!

YOUR VIRGINITY

BREEDS MITES,

*much like*

*a cheese*

*away,*

YOU THREE-INCH FOOL!

THE TAMING OF THE SHREW, ACT 4, SCENE 1

THOU FLEA,

THOU NIT,

THOU WINTER-CRICKET

THOU!

THOU ART UNFIT

FOR ANY PLACE

*but hell*

RICHARD III, ACT 1, SCENE 2

# insult generator

| A | B | C |
| --- | --- | --- |
| ARTLESS | BAT-FOWLING | BAGGAGE |
| BESLUBBERING | BEETLE-HEADED | BLADDER |
| CHURLISH | CLAPPER-CLAWNED | BUGBEAR |
| CLOUTED | COMMON-KISSING | CANKER-BLOSSOM |
| CURRISH | DISMAL-DREAMING | CLOTPOLE |
| DISSEMBLING | DOGHEARTED | CODPIECE |
| ERRANT | EARTH-VEXING | DEWBERRY |
| FAWNING | FAT-KIDNEYED | FLAX-WENCH |
| FROWARD | FLAP-MOUTHED | FOOT-LICKER |
| GLEEKING | FOLLY-FALLEN | GIGLET |
| GORBELLIED | FULL-GORGED | HAGGARD |
| INFECTIOUS | HALF-FACED | HEDGE-PIG |
| LOGGERHEADED | HEDGE-BORN | HUGGER-MUGGER |
| MAMMERING | HELL-HATED | JOITHEAD |
| BAWDY | HASTY-WITTED | HORN-BEAT |
| BOOTLESS | GUTS-GRIPING | HARPY |
| COCKERED | FOOL-BORN | GUDGEON |
| CRAVEN | FLY-BITTEN | FUSTILARIAN |
| DANKISH | FEN-SUCKED | FLIRT-GILL |
| DRONING | ELF-SKINNED | FLAP-DRAGON |
| FOBBING | DREAD-BOLTED | DEATH-TOKEN |
| FROTHY | DIZZY-EYED | COXCOMB |
| GOATISH | CROOK-PATED | CLACK-DISH |
| IMPERTINENT | CLAY-BRAINED | BUM-BAILEY |
| JARRING | BOIL-BRAINED | BOAR-PIG |
| LUMPISH | BEEF-WITTED | BARNACLE |
| MANGLED | BASE-COURT | APPLE-JOHN |

CHOOSE ONE WORD FROM EACH COLUMN, PREFACE WITH "THOU"

Made in the USA
Middletown, DE
19 December 2022

19331594R00046